S0-CJM-554

Editor in Chief
Ina Massler Levin, M.A.

Editor
Eric Migliaccio

Contributing Editor
Sarah Smith

Creative Director
Karen J. Goldfluss, M.S. Ed.

Cover Design
Tony Carrillo / Marilyn Goldberg

Teacher Created Resources, Inc.
12621 Western Avenue
Garden Grove, CA 92841
www.teachercreated.com

ISBN: 978-1-4206-5919-1

©2009 Teacher Created Resources, Inc.
Reprinted, 2020 (PO603023)

Made in U.S.A.

Teacher
Created
Resources

This book belongs to

_____

Ready·Set·Learn

2

Get Ready to Learn!

Get ready, get set, and go! Boost your child's learning with this exciting series of books. Geared to help children practice and master many needed skills, the *Ready·Set·Learn* books are bursting with 64 pages of learning fun. Use these books for . . .

 enrichment   skills reinforcement   extra practice

With their smaller size, the *Ready·Set·Learn* books fit easily in children's hands, backpacks, and book bags. All your child needs to get started are pencils, crayons, and colored pencils.

A full sheet of colorful stickers is included. Use these stickers for . . .

    decorating pages

    rewarding outstanding effort

    keeping track of completed pages

Celebrate your child's progress by using these stickers on the reward chart located on the inside cover. The blue-ribbon sticker fits perfectly on the certificate on page 64.

With *Ready·Set·Learn* and a little encouragement, your child will be on the fast track to learning fun!

Kite Tracing

Directions: Trace the kite strings from top to bottom. Color the kites and the children.

4 ©Teacher Created Resources, Inc.

Where Are the Trees?

Directions: Color all of the trees in the picture.

Wind

Directions: The wind wants to blow away the balloon. Help the wind find the right path to the balloon. Draw a line from the wind to the balloon. Then color the picture.

Object Hunt

Directions: Look for these objects in the picture below. Circle the ones you find.

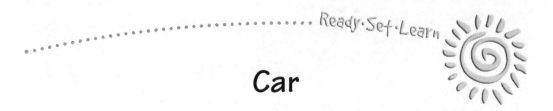

Car

Directions: Give the car some wheels. Color the picture.

Teddy Bear Alphabet

Directions: Trace the letters of the alphabet in order on the lines below.

Aa   Bb   Cc   Dd

Ee   Ff   Gg   Hh

Ii   Jj   Kk   Ll

Mm   Nn   Oo   Pp

Qq   Rr   Ss   Tt

Uu   Vv   Ww   Xx

Yy   Zz

Match the Stars

Directions: Draw lines to match the uppercase letters to the lowercase letters.

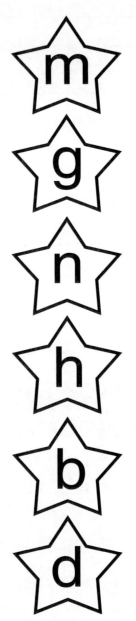

It Starts with a B

Directions: Draw a line from the bear to each of the pictures that starts with the letter B. Then color the pictures.

Matching Sounds

Directions: Match the sound to each picture.

b as in

c as in

d as in

f as in

g as in

h as in

j as in

More Matching Sounds

Directions: Match the sound to each picture.

k as in

l as in

m as in

n as in

p as in

q as in

r as in

Blast Off!

Directions: Look at the two pictures. Circle three things that are different in the second picture.

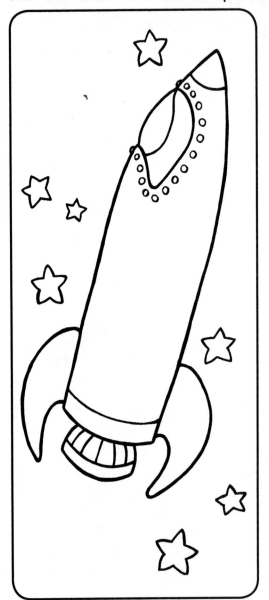
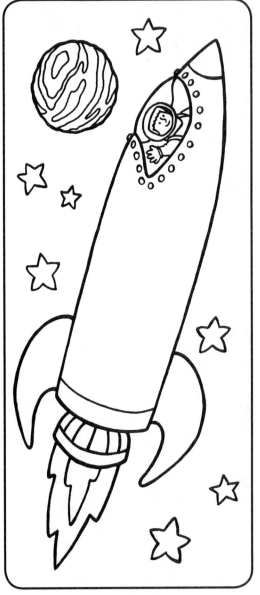

Hot! Don't Touch!

Directions: Look at the pictures above. Cross out the item in each row that is too hot to touch. Color the items that are safe to touch.

Circled Sounds

Directions: Color the pictures of the things that begin with the circled letter sound.

More Circled Sounds

Directions: Color the pictures of the things that begin with the circled letter sound.

Tracing Practice

Directions: Practice tracing along the dotted lines. Color the picture.

18

Who's Got More?

Directions: Look at each of the pet's bowls. Circle each animal's bowl that has the most food.

The Biggest Worm

Directions: Color the biggest worm. Circle the smallest worm. Draw a box around the medium worm.

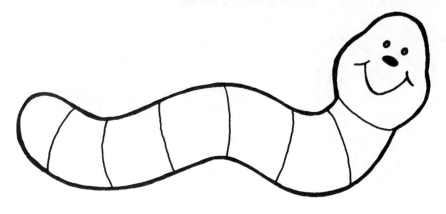

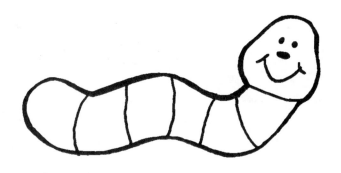

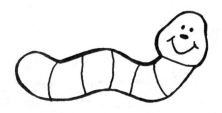

How Many Are There?

Directions: Trace the numbers.

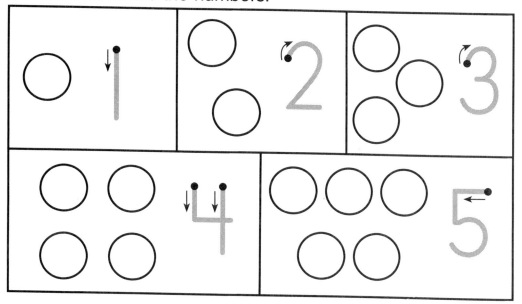

Directions: Count the items and write the number on the line.

LANGSTON

Count the Fruit

Directions: Count the fruit and write the number on the line.

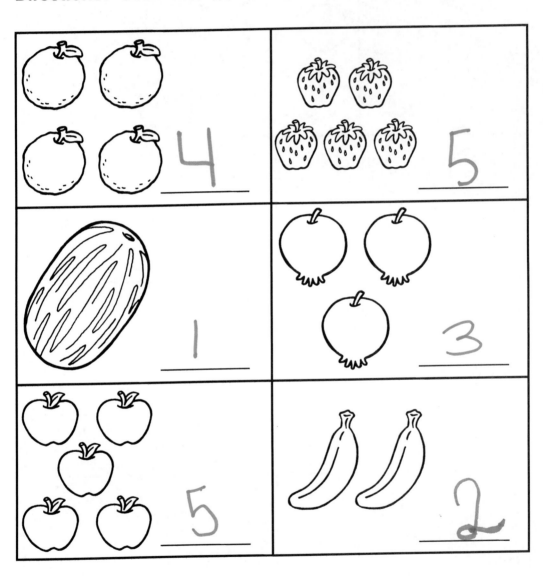

Ready·Set·Learn

Tracing Practice

Directions: Trace the numbers.

○ 1	○○ 2	○○○ 3
○○○○ 4	○○○○○ 5	○○○○○○ 6
○○○○○○○ 7	○○○○○○○○ 8	○○○○○○○○○ 9
	○○○○○ ○○○○○ 10	

Count the Flowers

Directions: Count the flowers and write the number on the line.

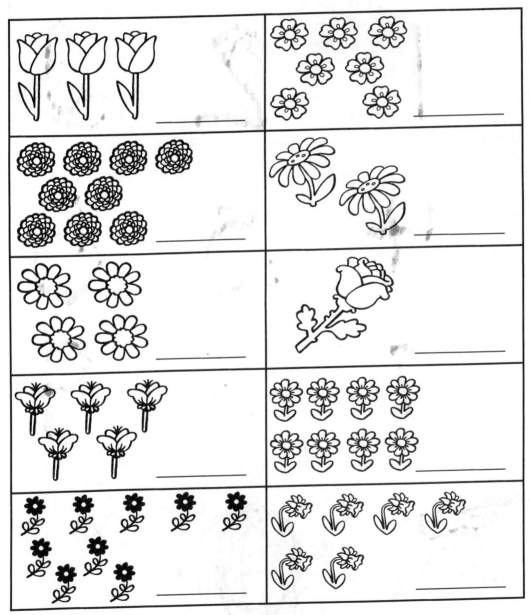

24

Where Are the Birds?

Directions: Circle all the birds in this picture.

Showers

Directions: Use the numbers to connect the dots in the right order. See what the bunny is holding to stay dry in the rain.

26

Expressions

Directions: Draw an expression on the faces in the boxes on the right to finish the patterns.

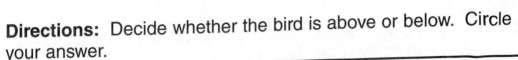

Above or Below

Directions: Decide whether the bird is above or below. Circle your answer.

1.

above　　*below*

2.

above　　*below*

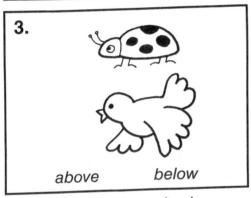

3.

above　　*below*

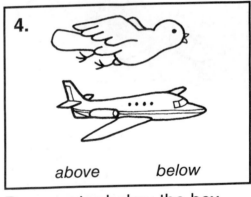

4.

above　　*below*

Draw a star above the box.

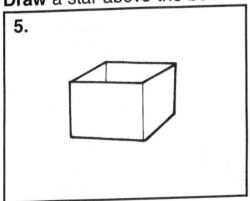

5.

Draw a star below the box.

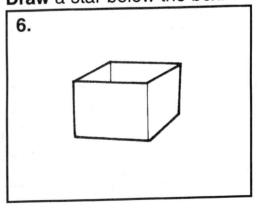

6.

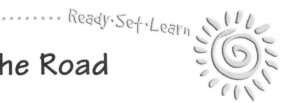

On the Road

Directions: Look at the list below of items to find. Count those items in the big picture and write the number on the line. Color the picture.

How many can you find?

Greater Than

Directions. Circle the side that is **greater** than the other side.

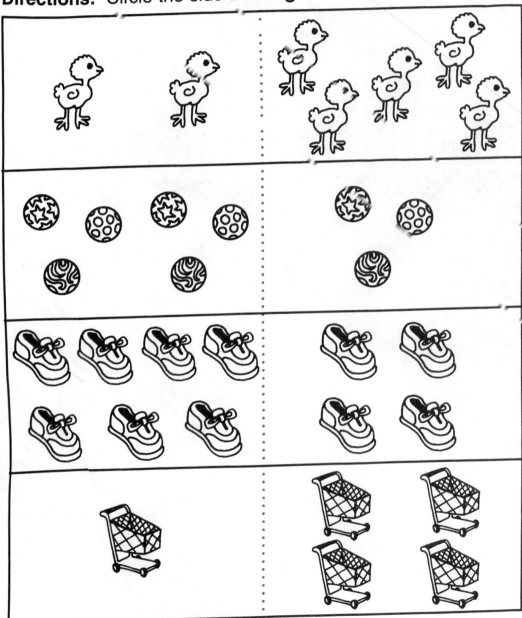

30

Less Than

Directions: Circle the side that has **less** than the other side.

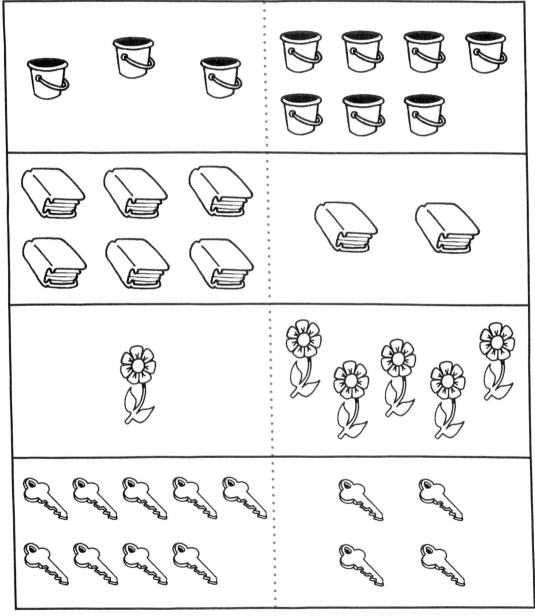

Where Do I Live?

Directions: Draw a line to match each animal with its home. Then color the pictures.

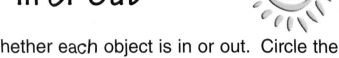

In or Out

Directions: Decide whether each object is in or out. Circle the correct word.

1.

in   *out*

2.

in   *out*

3.

in   *out*

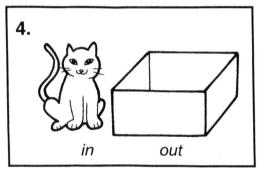

4.

in   *out*

5. Draw a star **in** the box.

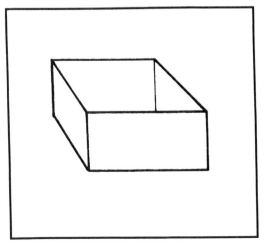

6. Draw a star **out** of the box.

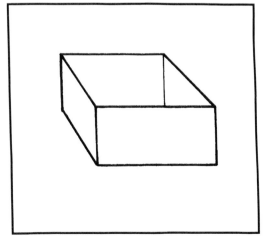

Find the Sounds

Directions: Color the pictures of the things that start with the letter sound shown at the beginning of *each* row.

Sound It Out!

Directions: Color the pictures of the things that start with the letter sound shown at the beginning of each row.

Laundry Day

Directions: Color the clothes *inside* the laundry basket orange. Color the clothes *outside* the laundry basket green.

36

Ready·Set·Learn

It's My Job

Directions: Look at each vehicle. Draw a line from the vehicle to the person who would use it for work.

Fly Away!

Directions: Color the largest balloon in each row red. Color the smallest balloon in each row blue. Color the other balloons green.

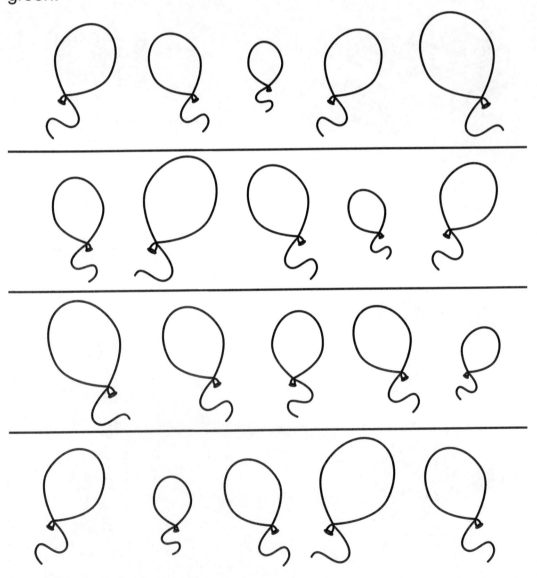

Mailbox Matching

Directions: Draw a line from each picture that starts with *m* to a different mailbox.

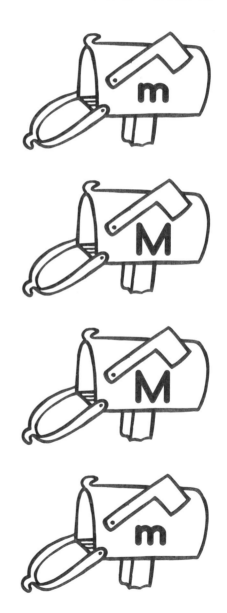

Plurals Practice

Directions: Draw a line from each word to the side it matches.

dog

dogs

cat

cats

bat

bats

cow

cows

40

Shapes

Directions: Trace the shapes.

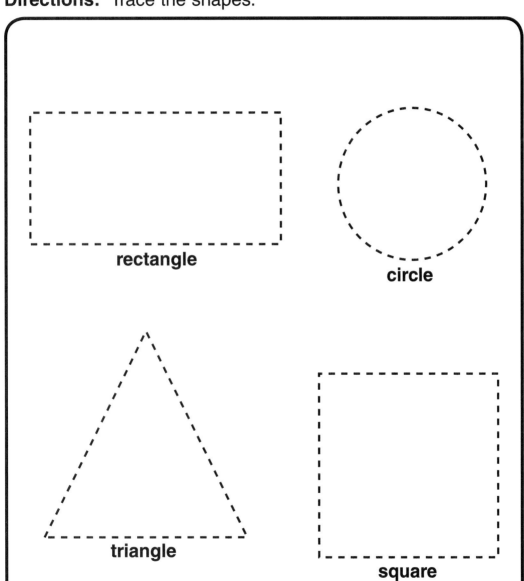

rectangle

circle

triangle

square

Circle Scene

Directions: Color each item that looks like a circle.

I found _____ circles.

Words that Rhyme

Directions: Draw a line connecting the pictures whose words rhyme.

Before and After

Directions: Look at each pair of pictures. Circle the word *before* or *after* under each picture.

before   after   before   after

before   after   before   after

Which is Smallest?

Directions: Circle the smallest object in each row.

Ice Cream Count

Directions: Count the number of scoops of ice cream on each cone. Draw a line matching the ice cream cone to the correct number. Then color each scoop a different color.

Where Our Things Belong

Directions: Draw lines from the things on the left to the place where they belong on the right.

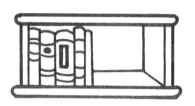

Animal Shadows

Directions: Draw lines to match each animal with its shadow.

48

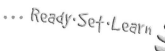

Opposites

Directions: Circle the opposite in each row.

happy	smiling	sad
up	down	right
little	medium	big
short	medium	tall

Plurals Practice

Directions: Circle the correct picture to match each word.

frogs

toy

balloons

book

Choo, Choo,

Directions: Each section of train track is numbered. How many sections long is each train?

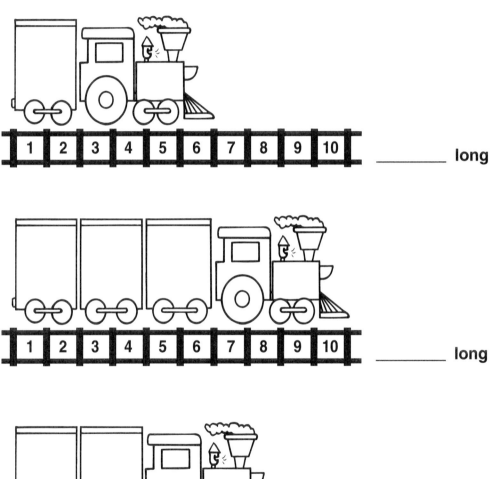

1 2 3 4 5 6 7 8 9 10 _____ long

1 2 3 4 5 6 7 8 9 10 _____ long

1 2 3 4 5 6 7 8 9 10 _____ long

Sequencing Events

Directions: Draw a line under the picture that comes first in each sequence. Place an **X** on the second picture. Draw a circle around the picture that comes last.

52

More Sequencing Events

Directions: Draw a line under the picture that comes first in each sequence. Place an **X** on the second picture. Draw a circle around the picture that comes last.

Letter Sets

Directions: Count the letters. How many in each set?

C C C _____ letters	h h _____ letters
r r r r _____ letters	a a a a a _____ letters
k _____ letters	m m m m m m _____ letters

54

Hot and Cold

Directions: Color the **cold** things blue. Color the **hot** things red.

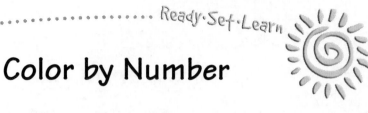

Color by Number

1 blue		**3** red		**5** orange	
2 green		**4** yellow		**6** purple	

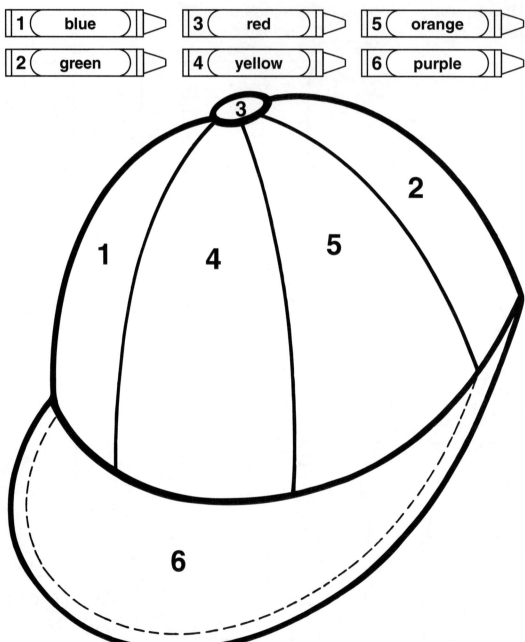

Set the Table

Directions: Draw a spoon and knife on the *right* side of the plate. Draw a fork on the *left* side of the plate. Then draw your favorite food on the plate.

People at Work

Directions: Match community workers to the tools they need to get their jobs done.

teacher

firefighter

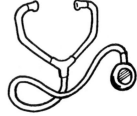

baker

nurse or doctor

58

Sequencing Pictures

Directions: Put the pictures in the right order. Write the number on the line in each box.

Matching Caps

Directions: Match the caps.

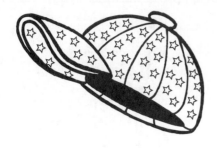

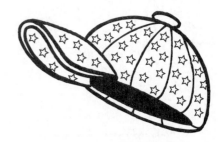

Where Are the Flowers?

Directions: Circle all the flowers in this picture.

Head to Toe

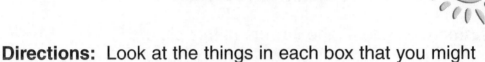

Directions: Look at the things in each box that you might wear. Circle the object in each group that does not belong.

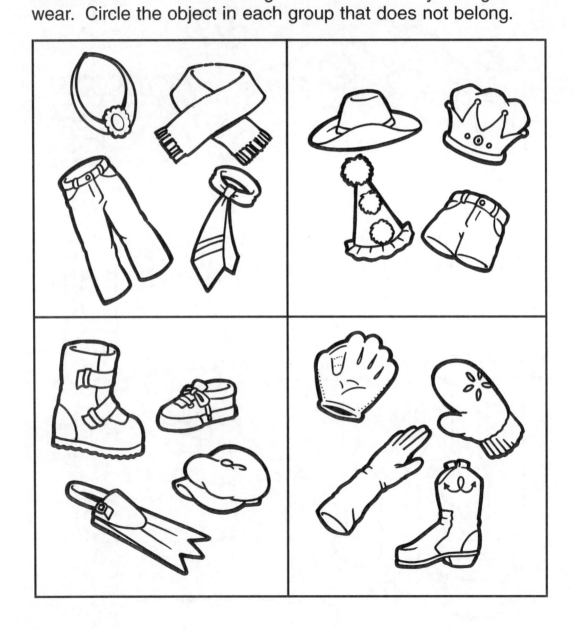

62

63

This Award
Is Presented To

_____

for

★ Doing Your Best

★ Trying Hard

★ Not Giving Up

★ Making a
  Great Effort